CHRISTMAS
Around the World

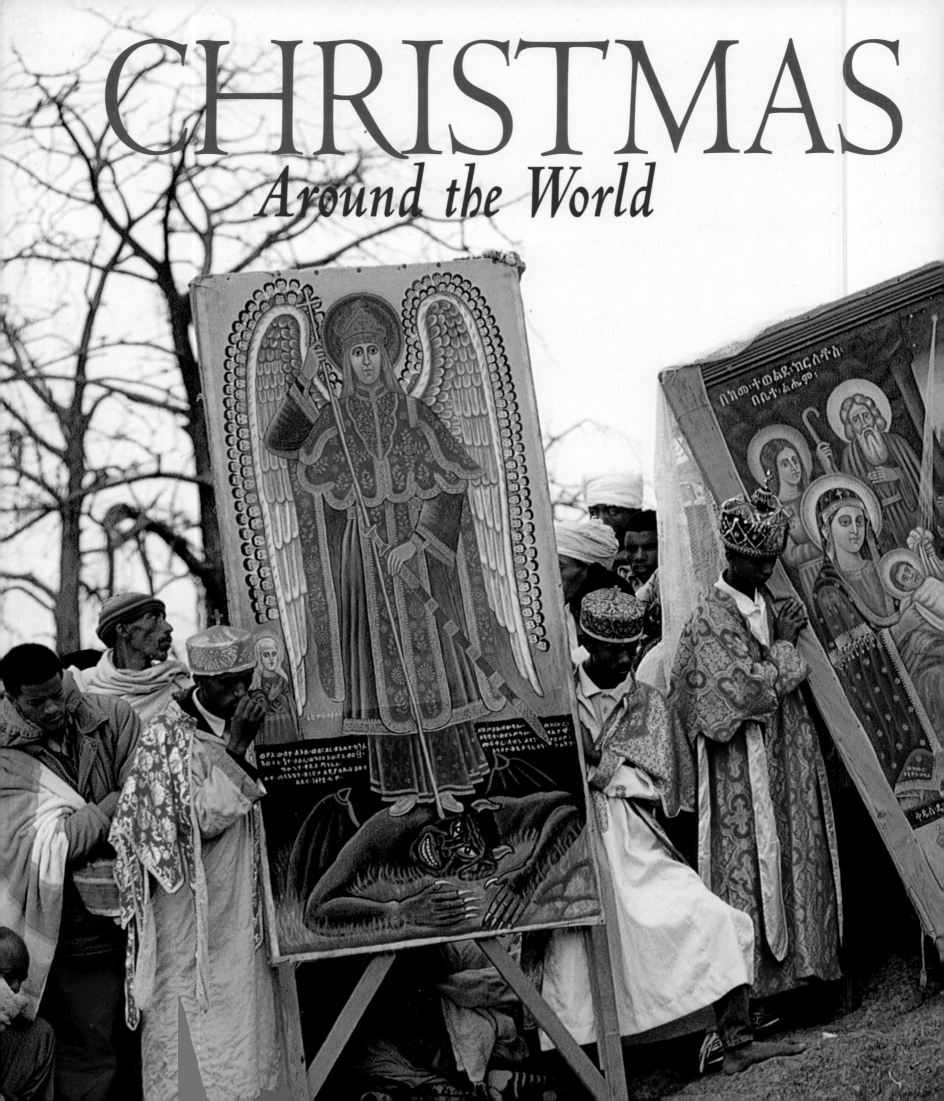

CHRISTMAS
Around the World

AN EPICENTER COMMUNICATIONS BOOK

CollinsPublishersSanFrancisco
A Division of HarperCollins*Publishers*

First published by

Collins Publishers San Francisco
1160 Battery Street
San Francisco, CA 94111

HarperCollins Web Site: http://www.harpercollins.com

Created and produced by
Epicenter Communications
Sausalito, CA 94965

President: Matthew Naythons
Vice President, Art Director: Alex Castro
Vice President, Editor: Dawn Sheggeby
Project Manager: Peter Goggin

Director of Photography: Marcel Saba
Designer: Ingrid Castro
Picture Editing by SABA Press Photos:
        Janet De Jesus
        Marcel Saba
        JoJo Whilden
Photo Intern: Ron Breijer

Caption Writer: B. J. O'Kelly
Chief Researcher: Sarah Karl
Research Assistant: Pamela Signori
Assistant Editor: Stuart Gottesman
Editorial Consultants: Dan Brekke,
        Spencer Reiss
Copy Editor: Merrill Gillaspy
Proofreader: Larry Lerner
Editorial Assistants: Rachel Glickman,
        Edward Smock

Library of Congress Cataloging-in-Publication Data:
Naythons, Matthew.
    Christmas around the world / Matthew Naythons.
        p.   cm.
    ISBN 0-00-225118-3
    1. Christmas—Cross-cultural studies.
    2. Christmas—Cross-cultural studies—Pictorial
works.
    I. Title.
GT4985.N33 1996
394.2′663—dc20   96-14875

Printed in China
First printing: October 1996
10 9 8 7 6 5 4 3 2 1

Previous pages:

1: A hand-carved figurine in Naples, Italy.
Photograph: Francesco Zizola

2–3: From Rome's majestic St. Peter's Basilica,
Pope John Paul II celebrates Christmas Eve Mass
for the 12,000 worshippers in attendance and
millions more watching on television worldwide.
Photograph: Angelo Turetta

4–5: Three icons of modern Christmas—
Santa Claus, a Christian church, and a gaily lit
evergreen—come together in Cologne, Germany.
Photograph: Manfred Linke

6–7: The Christmas season means warm summer
nights in Buenos Aires, Argentina, where the birth
of Jesus is re-enacted on the steps of St. Nicholas
of Bari Church.
Photograph: Gustavo Gilabert

8–9: Filipino schoolchildren savor their presents
in Manila, the largest city in the predominantly
Catholic country.
Photograph: Alberto Garcia

10–11: Coptic Christmas festivities in Ethiopia,
Africa's oldest Christian nation.
Photograph: Louise Gubb

This page: Snow covers a crop of evergreens at
Russell's Tree Farm in Storksboro, Vermont.
Photograph: Steve Lehman

THIS WORLDWIDE BOOK AND INTERNET PHOTOJOURNALISM PROJECT WAS MADE POSSIBLE THROUGH
THE GENEROUS SUPPORT OF EASTMAN KODAK COMPANY AND JAVASOFT

A Global Holiday

For unto you is born this day in the city of David a Savior,
which is Christ the Lord.

—Luke 2:11

On the first Christmas, the heavens stirred above Bethlehem in the land of Judaea. The rustle of unearthly wings startled shepherds tending their flocks. Angels soothed the frightened men and bid them attend upon a mystery: a newborn, an infant the angels called Savior, lying with his mother and father in a stable in the town. The shepherds obeyed and found Jesus, Mary, and Joseph in their poor quarters. Within a few days, three wise men drawn westward by a beacon star arrived to worship and bestow gifts.

Two thousand years later, the celebration has become a worldwide festival of spirit and light: a religious light that has flared across the centuries and lit every corner of the earth; the light that those in northern latitudes seek when the winter world is at its darkest; and perhaps the brightest light of all, children's glow of anticipation and joy. Christmas today, like Christmas of old, is a child's day, a day when all can experience again a childlike wonder in the world.

With *Christmas Around the World*, we set out to capture some of that wonder. In fifty countries across six continents, some of the world's best photojournalists put aside their own celebrations to record the solemnity of spiritual reflection and religious tradition; the spontaneous joy of community celebrations; the exchange of gifts and greetings; the mercantile bustle of the shopping season; and everywhere, the lighting of lights. To keep things up-to-date, we even used the Internet to ask people around the world where we could find the spirit of the season. The Web site will be updated annually with new photographs of international Christmas celebrations; you can find it at www.Christmas96.com in 1996, www.Christmas97.com in 1997, and so on into the millenium.

Sacred icons decorate a Greek Orthodox priest's formal holiday wear in Bethlehem.

Photograph: Alon Reininger

What the photographers brought back from their assignments during this Christmas season is a rich mosaic of the holiday in the modern world: mass celebrated by Pope John Paul II on the magnificent altar of St. Peter's Basilica, and Coptic Christian rites in stone grottoes in the Ethiopian highlands; an Arkansas home Christmas display fit for a theme park, and Nativity scenes lovingly crafted by Kenyan slum dwellers to reflect their own lives; the whirl of shopping in Japan's Kobe district, and the generosity of a Christmas volunteer who delivers gifts to AIDS patients in Boston.

A legion of miracles followed the first Christmas in Bethlehem. Perhaps the most profound in our age is how the yearning to realize the Christmas lessons of love, generosity, and understanding dissolves so many of our differences and binds us so closely together—both to our friends and family, and to our brothers and sisters around the world.

Merry Christmas, everyone.

—Dan Brekke

The little town of Bethlehem, now a city of 50,000 inhabitants, spreads out from the Church of the Nativity, a prime destination for the million tourists who visit the West Bank town annually. The famous white-stone church was built in the sixth century A.D. in Manger Square, atop a grotto considered to be the site of Christ's birth.

Photograph: Alon Reininger

● Bethlehem's Church of the Nativity is divided
into several sections, each under the jurisdiction
of a different Christian faith. Dressed in ornate
traditional robes and carrying sacred symbols
(*left*), spiritual leaders—including Greek Orthodox
priests (*top right*) and Roman Catholic bishops
(*bottom right*)— celebrate Christmas with services
inside the tiny church, leaving worshippers who
can't squeeze through the door to pack the square
and follow along on giant television screens.

Photographs: Alon Reininger (left, top right);
Ricki Rosen (bottom right)

● A statue of the angel Gabriel, who visited Mary to tell her she would bear the Son of God, is securely anchored in the Savior's Church in Bethlehem (*right*). Other Christmas story figurines are for sale in local souvenir shops (*below*), evidence that no place is immune to the mix of commerce and spirituality that marks modern Christmas.

Photographs: Ricki Rosen

● An Armenian woman offers a Christmas prayer in Jerusalem, the city that Christians believe was the place Jesus led his last ministry, died, and was resurrected. Pilgrims visiting Jerusalem during Christmas often walk the Via Dolorosa—the route Christ walked, bearing his cross, on the way to his crucifixion—and worship at the Church of the Holy Sepulcher, believed by most Christian groups to stand on the spot of Christ's execution, entombment, and Resurrection.

Photograph: Ricki Rosen

● *Following pages:* On January 6, Franciscan monks mark the Epiphany with the Procession of the Blessed Sacraments into the Church of the Nativity, complete with a movie camera to record every minute. The Epiphany—celebrated both as the date Christ was baptized and for the arrival of the Three Wise Men after his birth—coincides with Orthodox Christmas, so that several services are underway at the same time in different parts of the church, making the day's celebrations equal parts festive and chaotic.

Photograph: Ricki Rosen

● *Previous pages:* Outside St. Peter's Basilica in Rome, an elaborate manger scene vies for attention with a soaring Christmas tree. The Renaissance-era cathedral, designed in part by Michelangelo and Bernini, is said to have been built upon the tomb of Saint Peter. On Christmas Day the pope will appear on the balcony overlooking St. Peter's Square, where thousands of pilgrims gather to hear his traditional address, called *Urbi et Orbi*— "To the city and to the world."

Photograph: Angelo Turetta

● Pope John Paul II greets young worshippers during his Christmas Eve Mass inside St. Peter's Basilica. Until a fourth-century papal decree set Christ's birthday at December 25, a date that coincided with a pagan holiday honoring the god of the sun, Christians celebrated the birth of their savior on a variety of days throughout the year. The first formal December 25 observation of Christmas probably took place in Rome in about A.D. 335.

Photograph: Angelo Turetta

Although many Americans associate the Christmas season with snowmen and sleigh rides, the holiday makes most Italians think of sun-splashed Naples, the cacophonous city in the country's religious South, where an entire industry has grown up around the *presipio,* or Nativity scene. This Italian tradition dates back to the thirteenth century, when Saint Francis of Assisi is said to have created the first *presipio* in a village church. Most of the tiny terra-cotta figurines, made by skilled artisans in and around Naples known as *figurari* (*far left*), are costumed in the style of biblical times, although 83-year-old Vittorio Caruso (*above*) has for the past 40 years been creating *presipio* figures typical of nineteenth-century Neapolitan life—the time when the crèche scenes first began to spread from churches to individual homes. Many Italians add one new piece each year to their collections, which are usually on display from Christmas Eve until the Epiphany.

Photographs: Francesco Zizola

● While you would expect to see at least one *presipio* on display in most Italian churches, in Naples passers-by also find the tiny manger scenes in front of street corner shrines (*right*) and for sale in open-air markets (*left*)—leading city officials to boast that there are more Nativity scenes each Christmas in Naples than anywhere in the world.

Photographs: Francesco Zizola

● Part initiation rite, part raucous Christmas festival, the *Festas dos Rapazes* highlights the holidays in villages in parts of north-eastern Portugal. The details can vary from village to village, but in all cases the stars are teenage boys, or *rapazes,* who can take part only once in their lives. The boys are often segregated from the rest of the community for a short period between Christmas and the Epiphany. They emerge from hiding only after donning masks and costumes, usually carrying sticks in the tradition of Portugal's *pauliteiros,* or "stick dancers." The *rapazes* then go house-to-house bearing Christmas gifts, sometimes stopping to perform a satirical play—often inspired by real-life events in the community over the past year. At the end of the festivities, the boys are expected to remove their masks and attend mass, thus cementing their status as men in the local village.

Photographs: Cristina Garcia Rodero

A Christmas market spreads out before Germany's Cologne Cathedral (*far left*). Inside, a gold sarcophagus is believed to house the remains of the Three Wise Men, the city's patron saints, who gave the first Christmas gifts when they presented gold, frankincense, and myrrh to the Christ Child.

Photograph: Manfred Linke

Germany is not only the birthplace of such popular traditions as the *tannenbaum*, Santa Claus, and hanging stockings by the fireplace, but also of *Christkinder*, or "Christ Children" (*above and left*). Girls dressed as angels travel door-to-door in pairs on Christmas Eve, helping parents deliver presents to their children. German Protestants began this custom during the sixteenth-century Reformation, in order to link the giving of Christmas gifts more directly to the birth of Jesus.

Photographs: Ogando

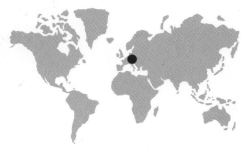

The holiday traditions of two countries meld along the border of France and Germany in the city of Strasbourg, which bounced between German and French control for more than a thousand years before becoming definitively French after World War I. Today, Strasbourg celebrates *Noël*—or *Weihnachten* to German speakers—with open-air markets and Nativity scenes that draw visitors from across Europe. As in most German cities, Strasbourg's market rises in front of the main cathedral, with booths offering crafts, toys, candles, and foods of the season—including regional specialties such as *bredle* (*above*), ornamental cakes which are used as holiday decorations. Streets decked with evergreen boughs (*right*) follow an ancient tradition: fir trees from local forests have served as the centerpieces of December celebrations here since the sixteenth century, when artisans set up their stalls near the cathedral to hawk their holiday wares.

Photographs: Marta Nascimento

Paris may be the City of Light, but at Christmastime it has nothing on Montbeliard, which, for 11 months of the year, is an unassuming French industrial town near the German border. In December, a brightly lit Christmas market rises in front of the town's St. Martin's Church, the oldest Lutheran house of worship in France (*left*). In this part of the country, *Père Noël* (*below*) shares the spotlight with Aunt Airie, a gift-giving fairy who wears a cape and is always accompanied by a donkey. Rather than hanging their stockings, like youngsters just across the border in Germany, eager children in France leave out shoes—preferably traditional wooden peasant shoes, or *sabots*—expecting them to be filled with treats by either *Père Noël* or *le Petit Noël,* the Christ Child, depending on the region.

Photographs: Benoit Decout

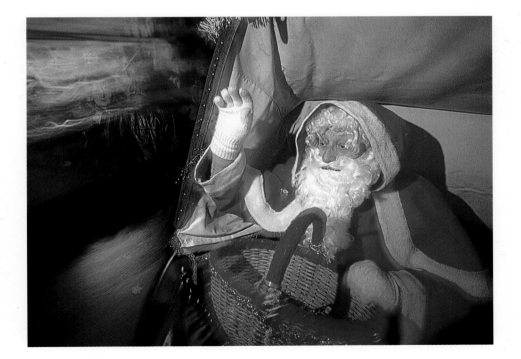

Beneath the more than 60,000 lightbulbs that give Montbeliard its Christmas glow, shoppers can purchase holiday decorations and the makings of the *reveillon*—the feast served after midnight Mass on Christmas Eve, which is the high point of the holiday season throughout France. The main course of the sumptuous spread varies by region: oysters and goose liver pâté in Paris, goose in Alsace, buckwheat cakes and sour cream in Brittany, and turkey and chestnuts in Burgundy. But the dessert is the same across the country: *la bûche de Noël,* a cake in the shape of the Yule log once burned in hearths throughout France during the Advent season.

Photographs: Benoît Decout

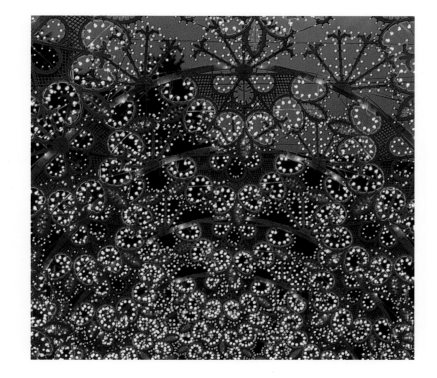

● *Following pages:* As it flows through the heart of Zurich, the Limmat becomes a river of Christmas light. In keeping with holiday tradition in Switzerland's largest city, children craft Styrofoam boats with candles inside and launch them in the Limmat—where onlookers line the banks to watch the handiwork float downstream.

Photographs: Thomas Hartwell

Santa Claus takes a rest in a store window in Zurich (*above*). In some parts of the country, *Samichlaus*—as Swiss German speakers call him—comes on December 6, the day named after Bishop Nicholas of Myra; the fourth-century bishop was later canonized as Saint Nicholas, patron of children, and is the forerunner of the jolly old elf himself. In a country famed for its neutrality, soldier ornaments (*left*) stand in formation, ready to be deployed to various family Christmas trees, which, in traditional Swiss homes, are not set up and decorated until Christmas Eve.

Photographs: Thomas Hartwell

A life-sized Advent calendar in the Swiss village of Nord Erlinsbach (*top and bottom right*) counts down the days until Christmas. The families in the apartment building each decorate their own window to correspond to a day in December. Every evening at 6:30 a different family unveils their window, and then serves refreshments to their neighbors.

Photographs: Thomas Hartwell

● *Following pages:* Candles punctuate the darkness at a cemetery in Espoo, Finland, where members of the Forsman family visit their relatives' grave-sites in the Nordic country's most solemn Christmas Eve custom. A few hours later, the laughter of children will pierce the night air as Father Christmas goes house-to-house to hand out presents. After Christmas Eve dinner, the adults traditionally enjoy a moment of peace in the sauna.

Photograph: Jonathan Olley

Christmas Eve is truly a silent night for 30 people walking from the Belgian city of Antwerp to the village of Viersel, about 15 miles away. Participants in the March of Silence, led by Jesuit priest Luc Zersteylen, introduce themselves before leaving Antwerp at six o'clock in the evening, and say nothing more until they reach Oelegem, 11 miles down the road. There, under a canal bridge, they join hands in a circle (*top left*) and take turns reading Bible verses aloud. The quiet descends once more as they trudge on to Viersel, where Father Zersteylen washes their aching feet in tubs of hot water (*middle left*). The priest then blesses their Christmas dinner (*bottom left*), which features bread and cheese and—finally—conversation. "Because the world is full of consumption," says Father Zersteylen of the annual march, which he first led in 1970, "we look for soberness. Because the world is torn by competition, we look for solidarity. And because the world is shaken by performance, we look for silence."

Photographs: Wim Van Cappallen

According to the Christmas story, a new star rose on the night of Christ's birth, leading the Three Wise Men on their pilgrimage to Bethlehem. Perhaps the image of that starry night has led to the central role candlelight plays in Christmas celebrations worldwide, including that in the Dutch town of Gouda (*right*)—world-famous for its local cheese but also home to Holland's candle industry. On Christmas Eve, all of the buildings in the city center, dominated by the thirteenth-century town hall, extinguish their electric lights in favor of candle power. When the Christmas tree lights are turned on, the mayor reads the story of Christ's birth aloud to the assembled crowd.

Photograph: Rien Zilvold

Pubs in Ireland are closed on Christmas Day, or *Nodlaig*, but revelers find plenty of time to share a pint in the days leading up to Christmas (*left and below*). Even people who don't speak Gaelic are likely to be able to chant the traditional Irish holiday toast: *Go mbeirmid beo ar an am seo aris*, or "May we all be together again this time next year."

Photographs: Robert Wallis

A group of schoolgirls tries out some Christmas carols on Grafton Street in Dublin, the city's main shopping thoroughfare (*above*), while across town Santa Claus visits the Abbey Presbyterian Church Nursery School (*right*). Back at home, each family's youngest child is responsible for lighting the candles that decorate every window of the house. Preferably displayed in sconces made of carved turnips, the candles are meant as solace to weary travelers, in memory of Joseph and Mary looking for shelter. Many Irish families spend at least part of Christmas Eve walking together through a town or village to view these candlelight displays. Holly wreaths festoon the inside of most houses, symbols not only of winter greenery but also of Christ's crown of thorns. And in a tradition dying out but not yet dead, the bells of some village churches toll on Christmas Eve from 11:00 P.M. to midnight to mark "the Devil's funeral," a result of Christ's impending birth.

Photographs: Robert Wallis

● Wide eyes take everything in (*top and bottom left*) at the home of Harry Goodman, a retired Londoner whose household decorations attract children from around the city. Life-sized Christmas figures programmed to move and talk fill his living room and garden, while a flesh-and-blood Father Christmas—played in rotation by Harry's nephews—poses with young visitors. Admission is free of charge to the thousands who annually visit the "grotto," as Harry calls it, and kids can take home a wrapped gift for £1 (about $1.75), or a photo with Father Christmas for £2. Harry has given up trying to calculate how much the grotto costs him each year, but says, "Whatever it is, it's worth it just to see the kids' faces light up."

Photographs: Mike Abrahams

● Five-year-old Jack Lewis tries out a new pair of peepers on Christmas morning in London, while his mother, Hannah, and older sister, Phoebe, examine the rest of the bounty left by Father Christmas (*above*). The night before, children were careful to leave out two mince pies and a glass of sherry for Father Christmas, and a carrot for his reindeer to share, since the English St. Nick brings his reindeer all the way down the chimney with him. Although most British are famously fond of their holiday traditions, Ebenezer Scrooge wasn't the only Englishman to stifle Christmas merry-making: after becoming the "lord protector" of England in 1653, Oliver Cromwell banned any celebration of Christmas to show his disapproval of the revelry—often less than somber and sacred— that had grown around it. Christmas festivities began again after his death five years later.

Photograph: Barry Lewis

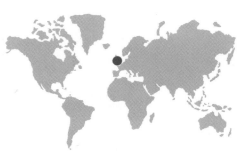

Mad dogs may join Englishmen out in the noonday sun, but even the dogs know enough to stay out of the icy waters of the boating lake of London's Hyde Park (*left*). A few dozen members of the Serpentine Swimming Club take the plunge each December 25 (*above*) in a 100-yard race for the Peter Pan Cup. The trophy is named after the most famous work of author Sir James Barrie, who first organized the chilly race in 1903.

Photographs: Jonathan Olley

Not all the hams in England are served for Christmas dinner: many test their theatrical skills in holiday folk plays. In the well-heeled town of Bampton, Oxfordshire, costumed performers go door-to-door, staging their play in living rooms and pubs as Christmas draws near. The plot, which has changed little since the Middle Ages, combines the Christian theme of resurrection with characters taken from the time of troubadours and fiery dragons. The central theme: a hero, usually named King George or Saint George, is killed by a dastardly villain and then miraculously comes back to life.

Photographs: Justin Leighton

Following pages: For most people in England, December 26—Boxing Day, a legal holiday—is a time to bestow gifts on the postman and milkman and to recover from the culinary excesses of Christmas Day. But it's also a day named after Saint Stephen, patron of horses, making it the ideal day for the annual Duke of Beaufort Hunt on the Badminton Estate in Gloucestershire. Thirty-three hounds lead members over the frozen ground in England's oldest foxhunt.

Photograph: Homer Sykes

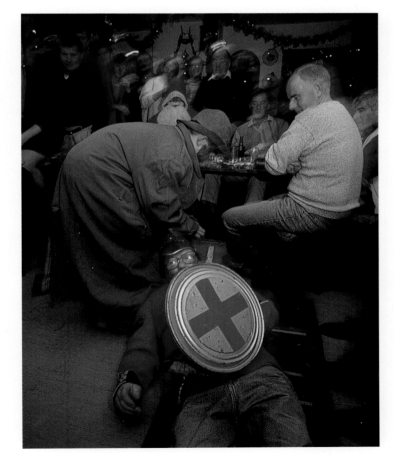

● *Previous pages:* Women wearing plastic to shield themselves from the weather add an angelic look to the holiday streets of Prague. In earlier times, Czech women, especially those still unmarried, looked forward to Christmas as a time to foretell the next year's events: a favorite trick in the countryside was to shake a tree or fence to trigger a dog's bark in the belief that a future husband would come from the direction of the barking dog. Similar fortune-telling tales, many of them centered on a woman's Christmastime search for a husband, are told throughout Europe.

Photographs: Antonin Kratochvil

● The public celebration of Christmas has returned to the Czech Republic (*above*), which includes land once ruled by Good King Wenceslas. The communists who ruled the country from 1948 to 1989 were not nearly as benevolent as the tenth-century monarch, and often used secret police to compile lists of worshippers attending Christmas church services. Today, many Czech families attend church services and later enjoy a Christmas dinner of fresh fish—usually carp—purchased in an open-air market (*left*). Served either cold and coated in gelatin or fried, the freshwater fish is a Czech Christmas tradition.

Photograph: Antonin Kratochvil

● The hope of peace on earth returned to the Bosnian capital of Sarajevo in late 1995, after nearly four years of war. Members of the multinational NATO force, which included soldiers from France (*above*) and Italy (*right*) as well as the United States, divided their holiday between festive and spiritual activities and military duties. The latter included making sure that jubilant residents, celebrating with fireworks (*left*) and even exuberant bursts of gunfire, didn't get out of hand. Christmas Eve services for Protestant and Catholic soldiers were held on bases throughout the country, with one minister praising the troops by reminding them that "Jesus did not say, 'Blessed are the peace lovers'... but 'Blessed are the peacemakers.'"

Photographs: Eligio Paoni

● Muslims join with Christians in celebrating Christmas as a time of hope at a midnight Mass in the main Catholic church in the Bosnian town of Tuzla (*above*). Hundreds of people of all denominations packed the church, while those who couldn't squeeze in waited outside in the snow. City authorities temporarily lifted the ten o'clock curfew to allow the mass to take place. "After everything these people have been through," says photographer Ron Haviv, "it was hard for them to feel completely happy. But the church was full of a sense of guarded optimism."

Photograph: Ron Haviv

● A simple cross stands guard at the Tuzla air base (*right*), home during Christmas 1995 for U.S. troops and other NATO soldiers taking part in the international peacekeeping force. As the holiday approached, the troops hosted a Christmas party for Bosnian children, singing carols with the youngsters and giving them a chance to sit on Santa's knee. Many Balkan children received their first Christmas gifts in years, thanks to an airlift organized by religious leaders in the United States. About 800,000 shoe boxes, containing presents donated by Americans and Europeans, were distributed at refugee camps, schools, and hospitals in Bosnia and neighboring Croatia.

Photograph: Ron Haviv

● *Ded Moroz,* or "Grandfather Frost," is the hero of Russian children, delivering gifts with his niece *Snegurochka,* the "Snow Maiden." For a fee, Moscow parents can arrange for a home visit from the pair, making them a common sight on city streets (*top right*). As part of the non-religious winter holiday insisted on by the country's communist leaders after the 1917 Revolution, Grandfather Frost and the Snow Maiden doled out their goodies on New Year's Day—just as the giant tree in the GUM depart-ment store in Moscow (*left*) was a New Year's tree, not a Christmas tree. Secular winter festivities, such as the annual ice sculpting competition in Gorky Park (*bottom right*), also helped to take the emphasis off religion. All of that changed, however, in December of 1990, when Soviet citizens celebrated Christmas as a public holiday for the first time in more than 70 years, and church services were free and open. A three-week Christmas festival began on December 24 with the incongruous sight of the Soviet Navy Marching Band playing the classic Christmas hymn "O Come All Ye Faithful."

Photographs: Nikolai Ignatiev

Children in Moscow may enjoy the big city's holiday hubbub (*above and left*), but some Russians prefer a quieter Christmas, in a country cabin rented from bearded woodsman Anatoli Vasilievich (*near bottom right*). There, they enjoy traditions such as dancing around the bonfire to purify themselves of sin in preparation for the New Year (*top right*), and having Vasilievich tell fortunes by the way a thrown boot falls in the snow (*far bottom right*).

Photographs: Nikolai Ignatiev

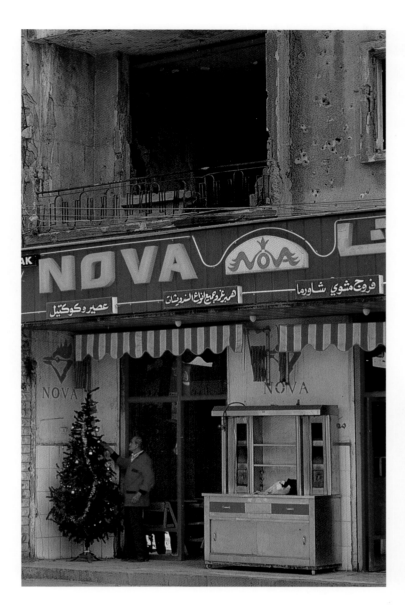

● In the Lebanese village of Deir el-Qamar, a Christmas tree stands watch over the town's main square (*left*). One-quarter of Lebanon's people are Christian, giving the tiny country the largest percentage of Christians of any nation in the Middle East. From the mid-1970s until 1991, fighting raged between various forces in and around Beirut, which was known as the "Paris of the Middle East" before the violence broke out. During the conflict, friendly relations between Christians and Muslims were shattered. Now, Christmas is once again observed throughout the country. Carols ring out from radios across Lebanon in December, and even in Muslim neighborhoods merchants use Christmas decorations (*above and right*) to entice shoppers—many of whom, wearing traditional Muslim dress, snap up tree ornaments and inflatable Santas.

Photographs: Norbert Schiller

Worshippers in Kenya, one of several East African countries with a large Christian population, approach a rural church on Christmas Day (*left*). Ninety minutes away, Christmas is more crowded at a church service in Korogocho (*below*), a poor district in the capital city of Nairobi. About 35 percent of Kenya's people are Protestant and another 25 percent are Roman Catholic.

Photographs: Mariella Furrer

Nativity scenes decorate the church inside and out in Korogocho, a slum area of Nairobi that is home to some 100,000 people. Residents make the crèches and carry them to the church in a Christmas Eve procession. Many of the homemade crèches are designed to look like Korogocho itself, complete with stagnant pools of water and mountains of trash.

Photographs: Mariella Furrer

In a land where Christianity was first embraced in A.D. 330, Ethiopians celebrate Christmas on January 7 with a pilgrimage to Lalibela, the holiest site for the country's Christians. The holiday, known as *Genna* to these East African worshippers, features processions of the Nativity and other Christmas icons through the streets (*left and top right*). On Christmas Eve, the faithful stay awake all night—their vigil fueled by beans and bread, illuminated by candles, and highlighted by singing, dancing, and praying (*bottom right*). The Christmas Day festivities culminate in a dinner feast, for which every family that can afford to slaughters and cooks a goat.

Photographs: Louise Gubb

● Even surrounded by thousands of others on the trek to Lalibela, pilgrims find time for study and reflection. Some worshippers walk days or weeks—even months—to spend the holy day in the Ethiopian village where thirteenth-century Coptic Christians built 11 churches underground to avoid persecution.

Photographs: Louise Gubb

● On Christmas morning, worshippers gathered at Lalibela share breakfast (*above*). Later, a cross is passed through the crowd for every believer to kiss (*left*), as part of a service that lasts several hours. The ceremony is held at *Beta Mariam*, or the "House of Mary" (*following pages*), one of the 11 underground churches that were sculpted out of rough, pinkish rock by Coptic Christians more than 700 years ago.

Photographs: Louise Gubb

Christmas is a simple affair for Christian worshippers in northern Bangladesh, the most densely populated—and one of the poorest—nations in the world. In a country where most people are Hindu or Muslim, Father Sondeep Bala (*near right*) tends to his flock with a mixture of Christian theology and local custom. Midnight Mass (*above*) actually begins at 7:00 P.M. so that worshippers, many of whom travel hours on foot to arrive at the mission in Haluaghat, do not have to walk all night to get back home. They return to church the next day for Christmas Mass (*far right*), which features hymns based on Hindu devotional songs, and round out the day with a lunch of barbecued pig served on banana leaves.

Photographs: Shahidul Alam

Santa's elves turn up in the unlikeliest of places—
even the lobby of the Delta Grand Pacific Hotel
in Bangkok, Thailand, where employees dress up
for the holidays as "Santarinas" (*above*). At the
Montien Hotel (*right*), even the spirit house—
a miniature temple for warding off evil that is
found in homes and businesses throughout the
country—gets Christmas lights for its twice-
daily salute by the doorman. Christmas is not
an official holiday in Thailand, where 95 percent
of the population is Buddhist, but Bangkok's
principal shopping arteries are decorated for
Christmas, and department stores run special
sales, gift wrapping included.

Photographs: Paul Chesley

● Santa greets his adoring fans outside a church in Caloocan City, the Philippines (*far right*). In the country that boasts of having the world's longest official Christmas season, the children have plenty of time to get into the festive spirit, be it in school (*above*), or gathering goodies from gift-giveaways in Manila's slums (*near right*). The holiday starts December 16, when outdoor Christmas lanterns made of paper and bamboo are hung; Nativity scenes are placed in homes; and the devout begin attending a series of daily 4:00 A.M. masses to ask favors of Mary and baby Jesus. These are dubbed "rooster masses" for their pre-dawn start. After Christmas Day, festivities continue until the Epiphany, on January 6.

Photographs: Alberto Garcia

90

In an encounter familiar to thousands of American department-store Santas, a pair of merry Wise Men frighten a youngster at the Casino Español in Manila. Spanish citizens living in the Philippines gather at the club on the first Sunday of the year to celebrate Three Kings' Day. This is the day that the Three Wise Men—not a red-suited Santa—bring gifts to good Spanish children, who, before going to bed the previous night, leave straw for the royal camels.

Photograph: Alberto Garcia

93

Santa may be a minor character in the world's most populous nation, but he still manages to occupy a position of prominence in front of the Friendship Department Store in downtown Beijing (*above and right*), accompanied by traditional Chinese lions known as "Guardians of the Doorway." Live Christmas trees (*left*) are also a rare sight, but artificial trees are big business: China is the world's largest producer and also manufactures most of the world's Christmas wreaths, lights, and ornaments.

Photographs: Adrian Bradshaw

● Christmas Eve is a night for lovers in Japan, where young Lotharios are expected to take their dates to special dinner shows, buy them expensive jewelry, and perhaps cap off the evening with a room in a luxury hotel. As the big night approaches, the streets of Kobe (*right*) are bright and full of shoppers. Christmas, or *Kurisimasu,* is gaining popularity as another excuse to exchange gifts in a gift-mad culture, but the religious significance of the holiday is mostly overshadowed in a country that is less than 1 percent Christian.

Photograph: Tom Wagner

The Nativity scene outside of a Catholic church 60 miles from Melbourne (*top right*) looks like a typical Christmas in Europe, as does the candlelit service inside a Russian Orthodox church (*bottom right*). But here and across Australia, "Chrissie" has increasingly become a day at the beach—where Oskar Kaze and his young friend, Gabriel Akira, look forward to a meal of barbecued Australian crayfish (*above*). Until a generation ago, most Aussies celebrated a traditional English Christmas indoors—even roasting a ham or turkey, despite summer temperatures that can soar above 100 degrees Fahrenheit on Christmas Day. After World War II, when immigrants came in waves from non-Commonwealth countries, the English influence began to wane. Christmas became less of a Dickensian proposition, leading to the evolution of a homegrown Australian Christmas tradition: a seafood barbecue at the beach. The government even got into the act a few years ago when it issued a Christmas stamp depicting a barefoot Santa Claus hanging ten on a surfboard.

Photographs: Emmanuel Santos

● Discriminating shoppers look for wares of the season at a December 24 market in the main plaza of Cuzco (*above*), high in the Peruvian Andes. Vendors sell rosewood, grass, and incense for home Nativity scenes, but the most popular items for sale are the crèche figurines—especially the *Manuelito,* the cherubic Christ Child (*right*). Most families in the Andes keep a *Manuelito* at home all year round, usually in a special urn or other place of honor. On Christmas Eve the figurines are taken to church to be blessed by the local priest, after which they are carried back home in triumph to take their rightful place in the family Nativity scene.

Photographs: Vera Lentz

Following pages: The most genuine *Manuelitos,* adorned with a mirror in the mouth and widely believed to have a heart of gold, are the handiwork of people like Georgina Mendivil, who toils away in her workshop making the hand-painted figurines from plaster and wood. Her best work can sell for as much as $500.

Photograph: Vera Lentz

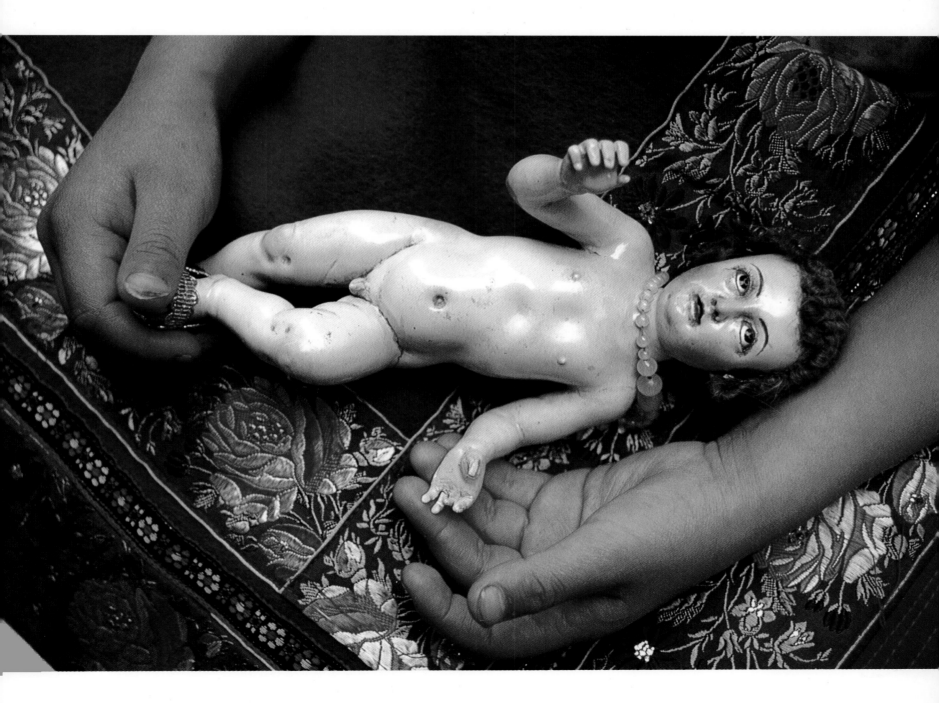

● On December 21, members of a Protestant congregation in Haiti gather for the first of five successive hilltop prayer sessions (*previous pages and right*). Led by assistant pastor Clovis Michel (*above*), they bring a Bible and water or juice for the daily four-hour sessions, which begin at about 7:00 A.M. At the prayer meetings, which culminate on Christmas morning, the worshippers "pray for everything," reports photographer Maggie Steber. "They pray for the health of sick loved ones. They pray for money: to buy food, pay the rent, send their children to school, build their church, and buy the seeds they need to plant or a calf to raise and sell. They pray and they cry. They stand to take turns giving testimony to God's mercy and love, and they raise their arms and sing hymns. They come here, they say, to be closer to God."

Photographs: Maggie Steber

● *Following pages:* Mournful eyes seek divine help at the sanctuary of Saint Lazarus, on the outskirts of Havana. A pilgrimage to the sanctuary to mark the saint's feast day on December 17 is an enduring Christmastime tradition in officially atheist Cuba, where authorities have begun in recent years to ease restrictions on religion. December 25, however, is still not recognized as a holiday in the Caribbean island nation.

Photograph: Antonin Kratochvil

● Food preparation is underway for the Chavez family of Mexico City (*above*), where the patriarch, Ruben, has been chosen as his neighborhood's *posadero* for the day in Mexico's most enduring Christmas tradition: *Las Posadas*. Early in the morning, the *posadero*, or "innkeeper," visits the local parish church, where he collects a statue of the baby Jesus. The statue is placed for the day at a special altar the *posadero* has built in his home, and neighbors stop by throughout the day to help prepare food, eat, and pray at the altar (*right*). On each of the festival's nine days, a different neighbor serves as the *posadero*—a position of honor that may take 30 years to attain. The festival begins on December 16 and ends on Christmas Eve, its nine days symbolizing Mary and Joseph's search for shelter on their journey from Nazareth to Bethlehem.

Photographs: Keith Dannemiller

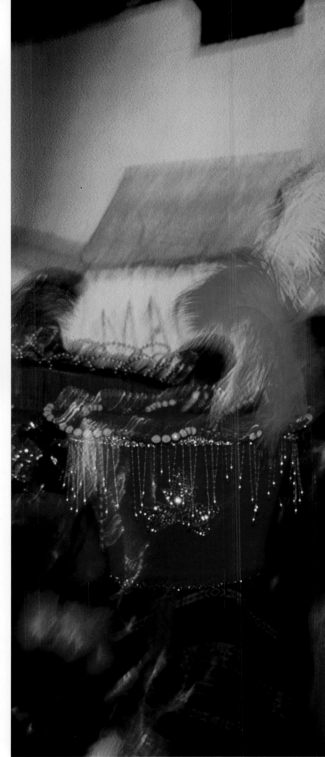

When evening comes during Mexico's *Las Posadas* celebration, costumed men known as *chinelos* (*above*), or "those that dance rhythmically," lead a festive procession from the *posadero's* house to the church, complete with fireworks and sparklers (*top and bottom left*). The marchers carry the statue of Jesus back to the church, where mass is celebrated before worshippers return to the house of the *posadero* for more food and conviviality.

Photographs: Keith Dannemiller

115

Seven years after it was planted as a seedling in Quebec, an evergreen becomes a Christmas icon for Timothy Leyne and his two young sons, Edouard and Thibault (*left*). Slogging through the snow and playing lumberjack heightened the family's Christmas spirit, says Leyne, who is one of a growing number of hardy North Americans who fell trees on Christmas-tree farms each year. "Now that we've cut down our own," he adds, "I don't think we could go back to buying one off the lot again." Back home in Westmount, a Montreal suburb, four-year-old Edouard fingers the fragrant branches he first saw adorned only with snow (*above*). "Once we turned on the lights," says Leyne, "they started jumping up and down and dancing around the tree. You'd have thought Santa himself had just walked into the room."

Photographs: Christopher Morris

Following pages: Christmas decorations spruce up the front window of a shop in the ethnically diverse city of Toronto, where the holiday touches Hindus, Christians, Muslims, and Buddhists alike. Says Rajan Diwan, a Hindu shopkeeper who is part of the city's South Asian community of about 235,000 people: "Back in India, very few people celebrate Christmas. But here we are now, in a multicultural society, and it's most important to us to celebrate Christmas." Coincidentally, the major Hindu winter holiday, *divali,* often falls near Christmas, so the festivities are combined. Diwan, who says the bright lights are his favorite part of Christmas, goes with his family to temple on December 25, where he prays to Hindu gods.

Photograph: Forest McMullin

● Bart Simpson skateboards over Manhattan as part of New York's symbolic kick-off to the Christmas shopping season: Macy's Thanksgiving Day Parade. The parade debuted in 1924, with the first of the giant helium-filled balloons added three years later. Now, a dozen or so balloons soar five stories above Central Park West and Broadway every Thanksgiving morning, each kept in line by as many as 50 marchers holding nylon ropes.

Photograph: Matthew Naythons

● As Christmas draws near, shouting is the best way to be heard above the chaos at FAO Schwarz's flagship store in New York City (*below*). About 50,000 people pass through the doors of the tony toy store every day in December—a far cry from the humble beginnings of the "Schwarz Toy Bazaar" in Baltimore in 1862. The store's founder, German immigrant FAO Schwarz, moved it eight years later to New York, where it had a variety of locations before settling on the corner of Fifth Avenue and 58th Street in 1931—and then across the street to its present location in 1986.

Photograph: Steve Lehman

● *Previous pages:* Evergreen trees, such as these for sale on Manhattan's Upper West Side, have been symbols of winter festivals for centuries, from the Egyptians to the Romans to the Norse to the Druids. The first time Christmas trees were decorated in the United States was probably during the Revolutionary War, by German mercenaries fighting on the side of the British. However, the tradition spread slowly and didn't become an integral part of American holiday celebrations until the mid-nineteenth century. The first commercial Christmas tree lot in America opened for business in New York City in 1851, featuring trees from the Catskills; today trees are grown and harvested in all 50 states.

Photograph: Mark Peterson

● Spreading joy to the world—or at least to Washington Square Park in New York City's Greenwich Village—carolers belt out Christmas tunes (*above*) with the help of musicians from nearby New York University (*left*). While today caroling is associated with carefree holiday fellowship, the history of going house-to-house through the snow to sing is a bit more grim: in nineteenth-century England, for example, many carolers were destitute and depended on tips generated by their singing to survive the winter. Carols are believed to have developed as a reaction by worshippers to the somber and often ponderous church music of medieval and Renaissance times—although few of the songs and hymns now in the popular Christmas repertoire are more than a century or two old. The best-selling Christmas record ever, "White Christmas," is a theological irony: Irving Berlin, the composer who pined away for a Christmas "just like the ones I used to know," was Jewish.

Photographs: Mark Peterson

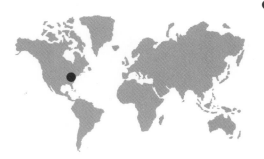

It doesn't go up until Christmastime, but the search for just the right Norway spruce for New York's Rockefeller Center can take all year—or even longer. Eleven years after they first saw this stately spruce (*left*) on the grounds of a convent in Mendham, New Jersey, Rockefeller Center landscapers finally convinced the Sisters of Christian Charity to let them take it away to Manhattan. The tree had been planted at the convent as a sapling back in 1931—just a year before Rockefeller Center had its first Christmas tree. With a public skating rink and several daily performances of the extravagant "Christmas Spectacular" at Radio City Music Hall, Rockefeller Center draws up to a quarter of a million people a day during the hectic Christmas shopping season (*above*).

Photographs: Mark Peterson (left); Steve Lehman (above)

127

Sparkling like a night star over Bethlehem, precious jewels for sale on Fifth Avenue top some grown-ups' Christmas wish lists (*left and right*). The gloves displayed at Saks Fifth Avenue (*below*) may make a more practical gift, but pearls and diamond engagement rings still lead the holiday hit parade. A tradition since the very first Christmas, gift-giving now accounts for about 20 percent of a typical American merchant's sales each year. The figure is even higher for jewelry stores, which count on November and December sales for about 30 percent of annual revenues. For the average American family, Christmas means a total cash outlay every year of about $800.

Photographs: Mark Peterson

● Life is good at Diana and Dick Beattie's apartment on New York's Fifth Avenue, where the couple's annual Christmas party was combined in 1995 with a celebration of their daughter Nina's engagement. The guest list of 48 included former U.S. Assistant Secretary of State Richard Holbrooke, who had spent most of the year shepherding delicate peace negotiations between Bosnia's warring parties. Seated among lavish decorations, which included nine Christmas trees, the guests sang carols between each of the four courses. "The most fun," says Diana, "was 'The Twelve Days of Christmas,' because we had six tables, and each table sang the parts for two different days."

Photographs: Mark Peterson

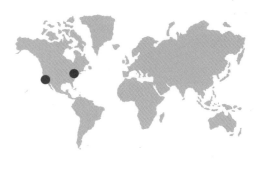

● The spirit of Christmas pulsates through Christmas Eve services at Zoe Ministries, a nondenominational church in New York City. "Artists gravitate toward Zoe Ministries," says Deborah Jones, a church minister, "especially from the black community." The church incorporates poetry, dance, music, drama, and mime into services because, Jones says, "the arts are very spiritual. They can be used as a tool for God's messages in an expression of the gospel through the arts." Perhaps the church's best known artist is Joseph Simmons—"Run" from the rap group Run D.M.C.

Photographs: Nina Berman

135

A volunteer for a Boston organization called Community Serving prepares to deliver donated gifts to low-income AIDS patients on Christmas morning (*above*). Some of the people who give their time at Christmas are those who don't celebrate the holiday themselves, says Community Serving's David Hirschberg, but "increasingly it's families with kids who have made volunteering a part of their Christmas ritual. Christmas has become so commercialized that the lessons of the holiday are hard to teach. Volunteering teaches kids that others may be worse off than they are and that they can do something about it." Children with their own long wish lists of toys can be sobered by the experience: "The people we serve tell us what they'd like for Christmas, and we try to accommodate them," says Hirschberg. "Often-times they ask for things as simple as socks. It's heartbreaking; just socks."

Photograph: Ed Quinn

● Young helpers serve the Christmas Eve pancake breakfast at the Bowery Mission in New York City (*below*). In addition to feeding the hungry—as many as 2,000 each day during the holiday season—the 117-year-old mission, a project of the Christian Herald Association, hosts an eight-month program of skills training and Bible classes to help homeless people and chronic substance abusers get back on their feet. Says Assistant Director James Macklin, "I always try to give and share what I can of myself. That's Christmas to me, and I try to do it every day."

Photograph: Mark Peterson

● *Following pages:* Bridget Loehn, six, and Danathy Reker, three, twirl around in their Christmas best at the Door of Hope, a transitional homeless shelter in Pasadena, California. Five families at a time live in a rambling Victorian home, each for at least three months. While the kids attend school, their parents receive intensive job training. "Christmas is a good time for the kids here," says the shelter's Jim Martin. "The families trim the tree together and eat Christmas dinner together. For the kids, it's like having new brothers and sisters. And their energy level is fantastic." This year, the celebration was heightened by the birth of a baby to one of the shelter families on December 22: "That's part of what the season is all about," says Martin, "new life."

Photograph: Lara Jo Regan

The motto of the First African Methodist Episcopal Church in Los Angeles is "First to Serve," and never is service more important to Reverend Cecil Murray (*far right*) and his massive congregation than during the holiday season. Christmas preparations begin in March for members of the church, which is located in the South-Central section of the city that was scarred by riots in 1992. When the holiday comes, the church's 11,000 parishioners participate by bringing gifts for underprivileged neighborhood children (*near right*); by helping to prepare the 8,000 food baskets given to the needy on Christmas Day; by attending church services (*below*); and by singing in the church's six choirs, which entertain at area malls and other public places throughout December. Reverend Jeanne Beharry, who assists Reverend Murray, explains, "This is how we make God's word real."

Photographs: Lara Jo Regan

Staff members try to keep spirits bright among the patients at Childrens Hospital Los Angeles (*above*), where, says spokesperson Steve Rutledge, "the kids are pretty spoiled by the end of December." Besides Santa himself, entertainers and L.A. sports stars stop by in December bearing gifts for the young patients—some just having their tonsils out, others undergoing chemotherapy. "Of course they want to go home," says Rutledge, especially in December. "But we make sure there are many reasons to be happy here."

Photograph: Lara Jo Regan

● Hoping that the Christmas spirit hits shoppers outside of stores as well as inside, a quartet of Santas prepares for a Volunteers of America (VOA) fund-raising shift on the street corners of New York City. Money collected by the VOA sidewalk Santas goes toward food vouchers for the hungry. For many of the Santas, some of whom are recovering drug and alcohol abusers, helping others at Christmastime is a way to thank those who have helped them.

Photograph: Mark Peterson

● Since Santa Claus became a department store fixture in the early twentieth century, the fine art of portraying the jolliest man on earth has become the subject of professional training courses, including this one in Alaska (*above*). Charles Howard started the world's first school for department store Santas in 1937. In addition to practical advice, like telling his students to lay off the garlic at lunch, Howard provided them with inspirational words that still hold true for today's would-be Santas: "He errs who thinks that Santa enters through the chimney. He enters through the heart."

Photograph: Al Grillo

A team of Rudolphs, red noses and all, performs a Christmas routine at the Brethren Retirement Village in Lancaster, Pennsylvania (*below*). The Grey Mermaids, a group of synchronized swimmers that grew out of a weekly water aerobics class at the village, annually sings and swims its way through a holiday pageant for townspeople and village residents. "The show is a great advertisement for the benefits of aquatic therapy," says trainer Roxanne Lloyd. "Many of these women have suffered from arthritis, knee replacements, or heart surgery, and the gentle movement in warm water helps relieve their aches and pains." The benefits are not just physical, says mermaid Laverne Bealer: "For women our age, letting down our hair and pretending to be Rudolph the Red-Nosed Reindeer can take away the cares of the world."

Photograph: Nina Berman

Everything is a spectacle in Las Vegas, where two Christmas traditions—bright lights and easy spending—are common year-round. So getting noticed at Christmastime requires something special: in this case, oversized holiday characters (*above and top right*) and a performance by the Garside Middle School Orchestra (*bottom right*). The occasion was the grand opening of a $70 million revitalization program on the city's famed Fremont Street, featuring—among other desert oddities—a 6,000-square-foot outdoor ice rink.

Photographs: Mary Ellen Mark

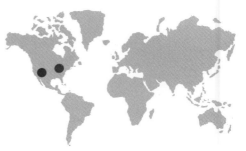

● *Following pages:* The names on their driver's licenses are Jerry and Dorothy Sheahan, but to their neighbors in Mount Pleasant, Michigan—even to their mail carrier—they are Mr. and Mrs. Santa Claus. And why not? Every year since 1970, the Sheahans have decorated their yard with seemingly endless strings of Christmas lights, adding something new each December. (Santa Sheahan stopped counting the lights a few years ago at 70,000.) Decked out in their Christmas finest, the season's First Couple greets visitors every evening from Thanksgiving Saturday until New Year's, making sure that no kid leaves their house without a candy cane. Their motivation, says Mrs. Claus, is simple: "We get great joy out of making people happy."

Photograph: Shelly Katz

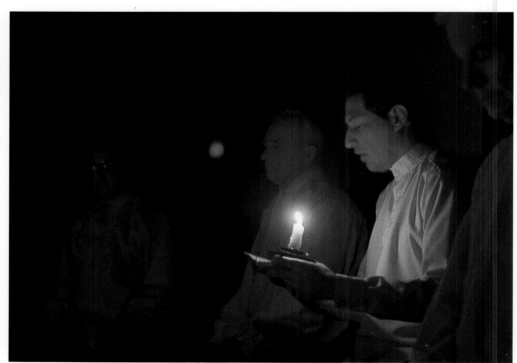

● A cross marks the Vermont property of the Weston Priory (*right*), home to 13 Benedictine monks. Over the holidays, the brothers decorate their home by bringing in greenery from their tree farm (*below*), while at their regular 5:00 A.M. prayers they light candles (*left and bottom left*)—a symbol of Christ illuminating the world. On Christmas Day, the brothers host a lunch for family, friends, and members of the local community—often as many as 300 people. Despite their monastic lifestyle, Brother Richard declares, "We like to be festive."

Photographs: Steve Lehman

Previous pages: A skeptical Cooper McLane, age two, joins friends and relatives for a sleigh ride at Russell's Tree Farm in Storksboro, Vermont. A pair of horses named Bib and Bob—with jingle bells attached, of course—carry visitors out to the woods to select their trees from among 10,000 in various stages of growth. Says owner Dave Russell, "We hear a lot of carols out here. Something about bouncing along through the snow in the sled makes people just burst out singing."

Photograph: Steve Lehman

The December holidays are an interfaith affair at the Vermont home of Larry Sommers, JoAnne Dennee, and their 11-year-old daughter, Brooke. "Christmas," says JoAnne, "is the story of a child, with the promise of love, being born into a nurturing world. It's about seeing the light, the spiritual spark, in every child." Hanukkah, the Jewish Festival of Lights, "is about standing up for what you believe in, even if it's unpopular, and teaches us that miracles are possible even when they're not physically viable." In addition to celebrating both Hanukkah and Christmas, the family has drawn on the importance of light and candles in the two winter holidays to create a ritual of its own—the lighting of a candle for 12 straight nights, beginning on Christmas, followed by a discussion of what JoAnne calls "the miracles in our lives."

Photographs: Steve Lehman

● Ann Roach, who requested a reindeer for Christmas, tramps through the grounds of the Minnesota Zoo with Santa (Don Mereen) and his reindeer, Cupid. Such an exhilarating day with St. Nick will probably leave no question in Ann's mind as to whether Santa exists; a century earlier, eight-year-old Virginia O'Hanlon had her doubts and wrote a letter to the *New York Sun,* saying that her playmates had told her there was no Santa Claus. Could the *Sun,* she wondered, set her straight? The 1897 response of editor Francis Church still rings true. Noting that Virginia's little friends "have been affected by the skepticism of a skeptical age," the editorial went on to say: "Yes, Virginia, there is a Santa Claus. He exists as certainly as love and generosity and devotion exist, and you know that they abound and give to your life its highest beauty and joy. Alas! how dreary would be the world if there were no Santa Claus. . . . There would be no childlike faith then, no poetry, no romance to make tolerable this existence. . . . Thank God he lives, and he lives forever. A thousand years from now, Virginia, nay, ten times ten thousand years from now, he will continue to make glad the heart of childhood."

Photograph: Stormi Greener

A visit with St. Nicholas is serious stuff for a Boston girl, who carefully gathers her thoughts before expressing her Christmas wishes (*top*). For four-year-old Matthew Lysy, the somber moment comes from trying to take it all in on his first holiday trip to FAO Schwarz in New York City (*above*). "He was so excited he couldn't sleep the night before," reports father Christian Lysy. "And once we got there, he had no trouble deciding—he wanted everything." At Santa's Village, 45 minutes up the road in Torrington, Connecticut, a young visitor takes in a display of the most popular toys from the 48 years the village has been in business (*right*).

Photographs: Ed Quinn (top); Steve Lehman (above and right)

The bane of any parent's Christmas—the dreaded present that comes in a box stamped "some assembly required"—stands finally mastered behind young Emily Quinn of Weston, Massachusetts (*above*). Her photographer father, Ed, admits he didn't get it right the first time: "I somehow managed," he says, "to put the first floor of the doll house on top of the second." The mistake corrected, Emily turns her attention to the next package and later shows off her tree-trimming skills (*far right*).

Photographs: Ed Quinn

Donning her own version of gay apparel, five-year-old Colette Page tries out her new makeup kit on Christmas morning (*near right*) before heading to a nearby hill in Westford, Vermont, for some serious sledding (*following pages*).

Photographs: Steve Lehman

When the children of the First Baptist Church in Weston, Massachusetts, dress up in costume to present a nativity play on the church lawn (*above and near right*), they're taking part in a custom that reaches back to the Middle Ages. Some details about the characters, now familiar parts of the Christmas story, were added long after the Bible was written. For example, the names of the Wise Men, Melchior, Caspar, and Balthazar, don't appear in the Bible—nor does it say definitively that there were three. Nativity plays have made a comeback in recent years: members of the First Baptist Church started theirs in 1992, says a mother of three of the Christmas actors, "to get the children and the community involved in something more important than Santa and shopping."

Photographs: Ed Quinn

● At Faith United Methodist Church's Christmas
Eve candlelight service in Burlington, Vermont,
teenagers read aloud from the books of Luke and
Matthew, and younger children (*above*) play the
parts of shepherds, angels, Wise Men, Mary and
Joseph, and even animals. But the baby Jesus is
now played by a doll, after the toddler chosen
for the part the previous year climbed out of the
manger in the middle of the pageant.

Photograph: Steve Lehman

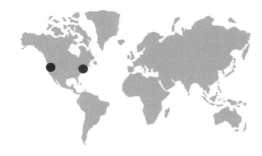

● The Christmas story comes to life on frosty December nights in the town of Leavenworth, Washington (*above*), courtesy of the Church of the Nazarene. The part of the Virgin Mary rotates among church members who have given birth within the past year, their infants playing the baby Jesus. The production features livestock from local farms, including a donkey that carries the Virgin Mary, and several sheep, goats, cows, chickens, and even llamas. Finding live animals is never a problem, says church secretary Marci Kirkpatrick, because "farmers enjoy their live-stock participating as much as parents enjoy watching their kids perform."

Photograph: Phil Scholfield

● Remembering loved ones they have lost, worshippers carry candles to the altar at a pre-Christmas memorial service sponsored by the Mount Auburn Cemetery in Cambridge, Massachusetts (*right*). Many distinguished Americans are buried in the historic, 170-acre cemetery, including Oliver Wendell Holmes, Mary Baker Eddy, Buckminster Fuller, and Henry Wadsworth Longfellow.

Photograph: Ed Quinn

● *Previous pages:* Against the backdrop of the Cascade Range, the Bavarian-themed town of Leavenworth, Washington, lights up for Christmas. A German-style craft fair runs in Leavenworth for two weekends in December.

Photograph: Phil Scholfield

● Bringing a little attitude to the role of Santa Claus at southern California's Universal City Walk Mall, Alfredo Ramirez poses for his own portrait (*left*) before climbing into his official chair, big enough to accommodate a whole family of kids at once (*above*). Donning sunglasses isn't the only way the age-old saint has stayed up-to-date: kids can now send their wish lists to the North Pole via fax or the Internet.

Photographs: Lara Jo Regan

Difficult as it may be for easterners and midwesterners to believe, some people would rather have sand than snow at Christmastime. In the southern California desert, near the Salton Sea, several hundred retirees live at least part of the year in RVs set up on the remains of an old airstrip, which they have nicknamed "Slab City"—and where Christmas means warm days and cool nights.

Photograph: Virginia Lee Hunter

● Young dancers take center stage as part of the Milwaukee County Zoo's annual Holiday Night Life celebration (*above*). For two weeks every December, the zoo hosts a series of Christmas events that include a tree-lighting ceremony, arts and crafts programs, nightly entertainment, and, of course, visits with the animals.

Photograph: Ralf-Finn Hestoft

● Christmas Eve becomes a fairy tale come true for Nutcracker ballerina Jennifer Cole of the Ballet Florida (*right*). Tim Lessig, Cole's boyfriend of three years and the theater's technical director, proposed marriage before a sold-out crowd of 2,800, who had been tipped off in advance that the curtain call would include a romantic surprise. The jubilant Cole, who responded by leaping into her fiance's arms, said later, "I knew what the answer would be the day I met him. I was just waiting for him to ask."

Photograph: C. J. Walker

● *Previous pages:* Too big for an Arkansas neighborhood, a spectacular Christmas light show fits right in at Disney-MGM Studios in central Florida. Jennings and Mitzi Osborne originally built the display at their home, but were ordered by the Arkansas Supreme Court to reduce it when nearby residents complained of noise and traffic jams caused by gawkers. Walt Disney World stepped in to host the collection of more than two million lights, including a 75-foot-high tree of lights, a 65-foot-high wall of angels, and two 30-foot-high carousels with 12 angels attached to each.

Photograph: C. J. Walker

Used with permission by Disney Enterprises, Inc.

● White tree lights twinkling in a Bethesda, Maryland, courtyard (*above*) were spotted by Bill Petros, whose photograph was the winner of the *Christmas Around the World* 1995 photo contest for amateur photographers. Petros, who lives in nearby Washington, D.C., says the contest piqued his interest "because Christmas is a very special time of year for photographers in terms of lights, colors, and images." Petros shot the tree from a variety of vantage points, and eventually submitted this image to the contest judges because the low angle "shows the strength and greatness of the tree and reminds us that Christmas itself is larger than life."

Photograph: Bill Petros

Dreaming of being a Christmas bride, four-year-old Charlotte Day-Reiss of Belvedere, California, shows off the veil from her favorite Christmas gift—a bridal outfit (*below*). "She's obsessed with weddings and brides," says her mother, photographer Anne Day. "She talks about weddings all the time and loves to pour through *Bride's Magazine.*" Charlotte even has the lucky guy picked out: his name is Sam, he lives in Miami, he is three years old, and he and Charlotte talk once a month by phone.

Photograph: Anne Day

Following pages: A low-tech version of Christmas lights called "luminarias"—sand-filled paper sacks illuminated by votive candles—are lined up in row after row across lawns and patios throughout New Mexico. Visual echoes of the Star of Bethlehem, they highlight the state's enduring holiday traditions, which also include miniature bonfires made of crisscrossed wood (also known in parts of the state as "luminarias") and the Christmas play *Las Posadas,* which re-enacts Joseph and Mary's search for a place to stay on the night before Jesus was born.

Photograph: Jim Argo

Santa doesn't have to travel far to get to Alaska, where a cabin in Kenai awaits his arrival (*above*). The state actually boasts a town called North Pole—so named because the temperature has dipped close to 80 degrees below zero on occasion—where mail addressed simply to "Santa Claus, North Pole" often arrives. For two-year-old Kalynna Booshu (*right*) of Gambell—a remote Eskimo village on St. Lawrence Island in the Bering Sea—Santa makes the short trip on an Alaska National Guard cargo plane as part of a program known as Operation Santa Claus.

Photographs: Al Grillo

On a cold and drizzly January day, Father Jerome Cwiklinski of Juneau's St. Nicholas Orthodox Church blesses Alaska's Gastineau Channel to celebrate the Theophany—in Orthodox theology, the day of Christ's baptism in the River Jordan. "We chose this body of water because a lot of people earn their livelihood out here," says Father Cwiklinski, who holds aloft a cross carved from a piece of ice. The cross was then sprinkled with holy water, replicating the baptism of Jesus. Historic and geographic ties to Russia have helped the Orthodox Church establish a strong presence in Alaska.

Photograph: Al Grillo

Jawbones from a 67-foot-long bowhead whale
serve to support Christmas lights glittering in
the mid-afternoon darkness in Barrow, Alaska.
Festivals dating back to the pre-Christian era
have celebrated the return of light and the
lengthening of days beginning December 22.
The Christmas Day sun never rises in Barrow,
the northernmost point in the United States.

Photograph: Al Grillo

186

Contributors

Director of Photography/Marcel Saba
Marcel Saba began his photo agency career in 1979 at Gamma Liaison where he worked for seven years, eventually assuming the position of Assistant to the Director. From 1986 to 1989, he worked as Deputy Director at Picture Group and was promoted to the position of Director in 1989. Saba opened his own agency, SABA Press Photos, in 1989 with a core group of 20 photographers, and affiliations with several European concerns (R.E.A. in France, Contrasto photo agency in Italy, and Katz Pictures in England). Now representing some 25 photographers, SABA Press Photos specializes in news, photojournalism, portraiture, and reportage, as well as corporate and advertising photography. SABA Press Photos is based in New York.

Art Director/Alex Castro
Alex Castro's career includes book and exhibition design as well as innovative work in sculpture and architecture. In 1977, he founded CASTRO/ARTS, a firm specializing in design for the arts. He has designed more than 100 photography and art books and museum exhibitions, including the exhibitions and accompanying books for the Corcoran Gallery's *The Indelible Image: War Photography,* for National Geographic's *Odyssey,* and for *Lee Miller: Photographer.* In addition to nearly a dozen exhibitions of his own work, his sculpture and drawings are in the permanent collections of several museums. In 1992, he designed the American Visionary Art Museum in Baltimore. He is presently working on museum projects in Kuwait, Jordan, and Ghana.

Photographers

Mike Abrahams
A native of the U.K., Mike Abrahams has covered political and social upheavals in his homeland and around the world. His photographs from Northern Ireland appear in the 1989 book *Still War,* and he has covered stories on migrancy in South Africa, the Orthodox in Israel, and the collapse of communism in Eastern Europe. Abrahams co-founded the Network Photographers Agency.

Shahidul Alam
Founder of the Drik Picture Library and the Bangladesh Photographic Institute, Alam is widely regarded as one of Bangladesh's foremost photojournalists. Winner of numerous awards, including the prestigious Mother Jones International Award for Documentary Photography and the Commonwealth Photography Award, his work has been featured in dozens of books and numerous magazines.

Jim Argo
A veteran of 30 years with *The Daily Oklahoman* in Oklahoma City, Argo has covered local and national news stories, major college and professional sports, and ten national political conventions. His work has appeared in *Time, Newsweek, US News & World Report, National Geographic,* and *Business Week.* Argo's work has been displayed in the National Gallery of Art as part of the Georgia O'Keefe exhibit and he has authored and contributed to several books pertaining to Oklahoma history.

Nina Berman
Nina Berman's work has been widely published in the U.S. and in Europe in *Time, Newsweek, People, Fortune, Money, Spin, The Independent,* and *The London Sunday Times.* She won two 1993 Picture of the Year awards for her work on Bosnia and for a magazine picture story on beauty and the American dream. In the last year she has documented subjects ranging from the American militia movement and the rise of the radical right to the daily dramas of a Broadway diva. Berman is a photojournalist in New York City with the picture agency Sipa Press.

Adrian Peter Bradshaw
With an academic background in Chinese, Bradshaw has been covering the changes in the world's most populated country for more than a decade. A native of England, Bradshaw's work has appeared in *Newsweek, Time, The Independent,* and *The New York Times,* among other major publications. Bradshaw is currently represented by SABA Press Photos.

Paul Chesley
Chesley divides his time between photojournalism, corporate, and advertising photography. A freelancer with the National Geographic Society since 1975, he is also a frequent contributor to *Fortune, Geo, Travel & Leisure, Life,* and *Stern,* and has had solo exhibitions of his work in museums in London, Tokyo, and New York.

Keith Dannemiller
Based in Mexico City since 1987, Dannemiller has had his photographs published regularly in *Time, Newsweek,* and *The New York Times,* among other major publications. Dannemiller has been documenting the daily life of Guatemalans in the *Nueva Libertad* refugee camp in the Mexican state of Chiapas for the past three years. He is represented by SABA Press Photos in Mexico and Latin America.

Anne Day
Day has worked in South Africa, New York, Washington, Cuba, Haiti, Japan, and the Soviet Union as a photojournalist and architectural photographer. Her work has appeared in *Time, The New York Times, Vogue,* and *The Washington Post,* and she has had several books of her architectural photographs published. She now lives in Belvedere, California, with her husband and three children.

Benoît Decout
Decout specializes in portraiture and corporate photojournalism. For the last eight years, he has been associated with the R.E.A. agency in Paris, and has photographed for many of Europe's largest companies. Decout's work has appeared in numerous magazines, and has been featured in international exhibitions.

Mariella Furrer
Based in Kenya, Mariella Furrer has spent the last three years covering the war in Rwanda and photographing the street children of Nairobi. A graduate of the International Center of Photography's photojournalism program, she has covered stories throughout East and Central Africa. She is represented by SABA Press Photos.

Alberto Garcia
Garcia is an award-winning photojournalist based in the Philippines. His work has appeared in *Time* and *Newsweek,* as well as in dozens of international news magazines. Represented by SABA Press Photos, his work has also been used to promote the group Children's International.

Gustavo Gilabert
Based in Buenos Aires, Gilabert has documented more than a decade of political transformation in Argentina. His photographs have been published in *The Independent, Geo, Newsweek, Time, The Observer,* and other major magazines. He has received World Press Photo, Fotofest, and Picture of the Year awards, and is currently represented internationally by the New York agency J.B. Pictures.

Stormi Greener
A two-time Pulitzer Prize finalist, Greener is an award-winning photojournalist for the Minneapolis *Star Tribune.* For more than twenty years, she has been covering the plight of the world's refugees, as well as a variety of social issues in the United States. Greener is a frequent lecturer at the National Press Photographer Association's seminars and teaches at the University of Missouri Workshops.

Al Grillo
Chief photographer for the *Anchorage Times* until 1993, Grillo has covered major stories across Alaska, including the Exxon Valdez oil spill and the annual Iditarod sled dog race. His work has appeared in numerous publications including *Time, Newsweek, Outside Magazine,* and *Alaska Magazine,* and he has won several local and national awards. He is represented by SABA Press Photos.

Louise Gubb
Gubb began her career in photojournalism with a project on Beirut and the Palestinian refugees. She went on to document Zimbabwe's independence, the last four years of the Rhodesian war, and the fall of the Duvalier regime in Haiti. For the past ten years, Gubb has been covering the socio-political developments in South Africa. Gubb's work has been published in leading newspapers and magazines around the world.

Thomas Hartwell
Hartwell has been covering regional news in Cairo, Egypt, since 1979. He first worked for UPI, CBS, and NBC, then as a contract photographer for eight years with *Time* magazine. Hartwell's work has also been published in *GEO, Newsweek, The New York Times,* and *Business Week.* He recently completed the majority of the photography for *Nile: Passage to Egypt,* an educational CD-ROM for children. Hartwell is represented by SABA Press Photos.

Ron Haviv
A graduate of NYU, Haviv has covered stories around the world and produced some of the first images of the killings in the former republics of Yugoslavia. His awards include a World Press Photo Award, Picture of the Year, and the Overseas Press Club Award. Haviv is represented by SABA Press Photos.

Ralf-Finn Hestoft
A native of Denmark, Hestoft now resides in Chicago. His work appears regularly in *Time* and *Newsweek,* as well as numerous other publications in the U.S. and Europe. Hestoft specializes in news and location portraiture, and is represented by SABA Press Photos.

Virginia Lee Hunter
Hunter is a contributing photographer for the *L.A. Weekly*. She specializes in documenting the lives of unique American subcultures, and has photographed the Blackfeet Indians in Montana, rodeo cowboys, and the traveling carnival circuit. A graduate of the Kansas City Art Institure, Hunter's work has also appeared in *Los Angeles Magazine, Sassy, Chicago,* and the *London Guardian.*

Nikolai Ignatiev
Ignatiev was born in Moscow and served in the Soviet Army in Afghanistan for two years. Shortly thereafter, he took up photography and moved to Britain where he joined Network Photographers in London. His features have been published in *Life, Time, Newsweek, Stern, Der Spiegel,* and *GEO,* among other magazines.

Shelly Katz
Katz has received numerous awards, and has lectured on photography throughout the world. He is currently based in Dallas, Texas, where he works as a contributing photographer for *Time* magazine. He has traveled extensively on assignments ranging from sports-action to glamour photography to industrial environments to fast-breaking news, and is a veteran of several *Day in the Life* projects.

Antonin Kratochvil
Born in the Czech Republic, Kratochvil is currently a freelance photographer based in New York with SABA Press Photos. He has covered assignments worldwide, including war-torn Afghanistan and Rwanda, street children in Guatemala and Mongolia, and forest destruction in the Amazon. His work has appeared in *The New York Times, Newsweek, Smithsonian,* and *Mother Jones,* among others. He has received the Infinity Award from the International Center for Photography, and the Leica Medal of Excellence for Outstanding Achievement in Documentary Photography.

Steve Lehman
Lehman began his career with the breaking story of the first contemporary unrest in Tibet. He has since traveled to more than 50 countries, covering events for *Newsweek, The New York Times, Time,* and *GEO.* In 1994, he was nominated for the World Press Photo Masterclass Award, and earned the Award of Excellence in the Picture of the Year contest for his work in Rwanda. He is represented by SABA Press Photos.

Justin Leighton
A member of London's Network Photographers Agency for six years, Leighton's major international stories include the famine in the Sudan, pollution in Silesia, the Kurds fleeing from Iraq to Iran, and the fall of the Eastern bloc.

Vera Lentz
Lentz was born in Peru and has lived in Europe and the United States. She freelances for major U.S. and international publications, and is associated with the Black Star photo agency.

Barry Lewis
Lewis' photographic work spans news, portraiture, in-depth reportage, and slick color promotions. His work has appeared in most of the world's leading magazines as well as in the corporate and advertising markets. In 1991 he was the recipient of the World Press Oscar Barnack Award for a photo essay on pollution in Romania. Lewis is a co-founder of the Network Photographers Agency.

Manfred Linke
Linke has been working as a freelance photographer and cameraman in his native Germany for more than 15 years, and founded the Laif Agency together with three other photographers in 1981. Much of his work has concentrated on the subjects of ecology and development policy in Brazil, and he has published several books about the city of Cologne.

Mary Ellen Mark
Mark has achieved worldwide visibility through her numerous photo-essays and portraits in such magazines as *Fortune, GQ, Harpers Bazaar, Life, Mirabella, Rolling Stone, The New York Times Magazine, Vogue, Stern,* and *The London Sunday Times Magazine.* She has been awarded the John Simon Guggenheim Fellowship, the Matrix Award, a World press Award for Outstanding Body of Work Throughout the Years, two Robert F. Kennedy Awards, and many others. She has published nine books including *Indian Circus, Mother Teresa's Mission of Charity in Calcutta,* and *Streetwise.* Mark's photographs have been exhibited worldwide and a retrospective, "Mary Ellen Mark: Twenty-five Years," is currently on international tour.

Forest McMullin
McMullin has been a freelance commercial and editorial photographer since 1980 and is now a contract photographer with Black Star. His work has appeared in *Time, Audubon, USA Today, Forbes, Scientific American, Esquire,* and *People.*

Christopher Morris
Born in Ottawa, Morris has worked for a variety of Canadian and international clients including *Time, Newsweek, Stern,* and *L'Express.* He has been represented by SABA Press Photos for five years and currently resides in Montreal, Canada.

Marta Nascimento
Nascimento began her career as a freelance photographer in her native Brazil, shooting subjects such as forest devastation and social movements in the Amazonia region. In 1990, she moved to Europe and joined the Paris-based CEDRI agency, for whom she traveled to Latin America several times. In 1994, she joined the R.E.A. agency, and covers social news and international feature stories.

Matthew Naythons
Prior to founding Epicenter Communications, Dr. Naythons led parallel lives— working shifts in hospital emergency rooms and traveling around the world as an award-winning photojournalist for *Time* magazine. He covered the fall of Saigon, the Jonestown massacre, and the Nicaraguan revolution, among other stories.

Ogando
The son of a German father and Spanish mother, Ogando first studied photo design in Dortmund, Germany. He now works as a freelance photo designer in journalism and advertising and has been a member of the Laif Agency since 1993.

Jonathan Olley
Olley is a freelance photographer and a member of the Network Photographers Agency. He has won several awards for his work, including a Nikon Press Award, and the *Observer's* David Hodge Memorial Award for his work in war-torn Sarajevo. His photos have been published in such publications as the *Boston Globe, Paris Match, L'Express, Time,* and *Fortune.*

Eligio Paoni
A native of Terracina, Italy, Paoni began his career in photography in 1984. Since 1990 he has been covering international events for the Contrasto photo agency. His features have included the war in Somalia, and an extensive three year assignment in the former Yugoslavia. Paoni currently resides in Rome.

Mark Peterson
Peterson began his photography career working for Reuters News Service in Minneapolis, Minnesota, and later worked for Reuters in New York. His work appears regularly in magazines worldwide including *The New York Times Magazine, The Independent, Der Spiegel, Stern, Time,* and *Newsweek.* He is represented by SABA Press Photos.

Bill Petros
Petros, the winner of the *Christmas Around the World* amateur photo contest, is a freelance and commercial photographer. His work has appeared in the *National Herald, Current Newspapers,* the *Mini Page* and various suburban newspapers in Washington, D.C.

Ed Quinn
A regular stringer for *The New York Times* in Manhattan, Quinn recently returned to his native Massachusetts where he is a photojournalist affiliated with SABA Press Photos. He has worked on assignment for most major magazines and lives with his wife and three children.

Lara Jo Regan
Regan is a Los Angeles-based photographer specializing in both portraiture and reportage. Represented by SABA Press Photos, she is a frequent contributor to *Newsweek, Time, Premiere,* and *Entertainment Weekly,* among others. She is best known for her interpretive behind-the-scenes take on Hollywood.

Alon Reininger
One of the original members of Contact Press Images, Reininger won the Press Photo of the Year award from the World Press Photo Foundation in 1986 and the Philippe Halsman Award for photojournalism in 1987. His best known work has documented the AIDS epidemic, for which he has won awards from Kodak and the World Health Organization. He is a regular contributor to *Time, Life, Fortune,* and *The London Sunday Times.*

Cristina Garcia Rodero
A professor of the University School at the University of Madrid, Rodero has had her photographs of Spanish and Mediterranean customs and festivals widely exhibited and has won numerous awards around the world, including the Eugene Smith Prize for Humanistic Photography and the World Press Photo Golden Eye Trophy.

Ricki Rosen

Rosen has worked as a photojournalist for the last twelve years, covering such internationl news stories as the revolution in Haiti, the breakup of the U.S.S.R., the fall of the Berlin Wall, and the rise of neo-Nazis in Germany. For the last seven years, she has been based in Israel, where she has followed the Arab-Israeli conflict.

Emmanuel Tolentino Santos

Born in the Philippines, Santos specializes in ethnography, social documentary photo essays, and editorial features. He began his career in photography with the U.N. High Commission for Refugees in the Philippines. He then migrated to Australia in 1982 where he became a freelance photographer. His work is in permanent collections in the National Library of Australia, the National Gallery of Victoria, Musée des Artes Modernes in Paris, and the Photographers Gallery in London, among others, and has been published in a number of books.

Norbert Schiller

Schiller began work as a photojournalist in 1984 in Egypt for Agence France-Presse. He was then transferred to Dubai, the United Arab Emirates, to cover the Iran-Iraq war, and later to Tunisia to cover North Africa. In 1990, he began working for the Associated Press and covered the Gulf War. Since October 1994, Schiller has been reporting from the Middle East for the German weekly news magazine, *Der Speigel*. He currently lives in Cairo with his wife and two children.

Phil Scholfield

Scholfield began his career as a newspaper photojournalist and picture editor. In 1986, he was selected as the "Best New Face" in magazine photojournalism by the *American Photographer*, and his story, "Sagebrush Country: America's Outback" for *National Geographic* was awarded the Magazine Picture Story of the Year. Scholfield's work has also appeared in *Life, Smithsonian, Fortune, People,* and *Time,* and he has five published books.

Maggie Steber

Steber has worked as a documentary photographer since 1978 and has produced major photographic projects on Zimbabwe, Cuba, and Haiti, where she continues to work. She has won awards from the Overseas Press Club and the World Press Photo Foundation, and her clients include *National Geographic, The New York Times Magazine, Life, US News & World Report,* and *Travel & Leisure.* She is currently a contract photographer for *Newsweek* magazine.

Homer Sykes

Born in Canada, Sykes has worked extensively on book, editorial, and news feature assignments for major magazines and publishers in Britain and throughout the world. He is the author and photographer of two books: *Once a Year: Some Traditional British Customs* and *Mysterious Britain: Fact and Folklore.* Sykes has also contributed to three other books, including the story of Paul McCartney and Wings. He is currently a member of Network Photographers Agency.

Angelo Raffaele Turetta

A native of Italy, Turetta began his career as a freelance stage photographer. He worked for a number of years with the Contrasto photo agency, and later pursued photographic projects on social issues, such as emigration, parties of the upper class, crime, and police corruption. Turetta has worked with both Italian and foreign publications and is currently based in Rome.

Wim Van Cappallen

A native of Belgium, Van Cappellen is a highly regarded photojournalist. He has documented the work of Medicins sans Frontieres, as well as dozens of news stories, including the spectacular eruption of Mt. Pinatubo in the Philippines. His work is represented by SABA Press Photos and R.E.A.

Tom Wagner

Wagner is a freelance photographer based in Tokyo. His work regularly appears in major news magazines in the United States, Asia, and Europe. He has covered the great Hanshin earthquake and the Hiroshima 50th anniversary commemoration, as well as dozens of other events throughout Japan and across Asia. He is represented by SABA Press Photos.

C. J. Walker

Currently a Florida-based freelance photojournalist, Walker divides his time between editorial assignments and architectural photography. He has worked for the *Miami Herald, Palm Beach Post,* and *People,* as well as other national magazines. His photos have appeared in several books, including *Santa Speaks* and *The Mission.*

Robert Wallis

Wallis has spent the past seven years based in Tokyo, Moscow, and London. He covered stories throughout Asia for *The New York Times* and *Fortune* and then documented the opening of the Berlin Wall for a *Newsweek* cover assignment. While based in Moscow, Wallis' stories included both social and political issues. Most recently, he photographed an Arctic oil pipeline spill and clean up near Usinsk, Komi Republic for *Newsweek.* He is represented by SABA Press Photos.

Rien Zilvold

Zilvoid is a photojournalist for the leading national newspaper in the Netherlands, *NRC Handelsblad.* His work has won numerous awards, including the "Zilveren Camera" Picture of the Year Award for his coverage of the Romanian revolution, and has appeared in several solo and group exhibitions.

Francesco Zizola

Zizola has worked freelance with Italian and international newspapers and magazines such as *L'Europeo, L'Espresso, Epoca, Newsweek, Stern,* and *The European,* and has covered stories in Albania, Northern Korea, Romania, Kenya, Yugoslavia, and Israel. He is currently working on the project "Heirs of 2000" about the condition of the world's children. He was awarded the MIFAV prize and the 1994 best photographic book award by the Museum of Photographic Images and Visual Arts of the University of Rome for a similar story on street kids in Brazil. In 1996 he won first prize for World Press Photo's "People in the News."

Thanks to all the families, individuals, and institutions who shared their unique Christmas celebrations with our photographers. And a special thanks to the staff of SABA Press Photos, who took time away from their own holiday celebrations to make this project possible.

Sponsors

Eastman Kodak Company
JavaSoft, a Sun Microsystems
   business

Contributors

Adobe Systems
Agenzia Contrasto
Arnowitz Studios
Cohen Publishers Inc.
Colorite Photo Lab, New York
Contact Press Images, New York
Fathom Pictures
Faulkner Color Labs, San
   Francisco
Federal Express
Impact Media
Internet Network Information
   Center (InterNIC)
Just Film, Sausalito
Kinko's
Laif Agency, Hamburg
Lehtikova Agency, Helsinki
Netscape
Odwalla
R.E.A. Photo Agency, Paris
SABA Press Photos
Sipa Press Agency, Paris &
   New York
Travel Advisors, Mill Valley

Friends & Advisors

Margaret Adamic
Dick & Charlene Alen
Bill Allen
John Altberg
Denise Anton
Harry Arader
Burt Arnowitz
Alan & Karen Ashton
Dana Attanasio
José Azel
Debra Baida
Marc & Marie Bailin
Sunshine Barcia
Kim Baskus
Milton Batalion
Andy Bechtolsheim
Pamela Bellwood
George & Keedge Berndt
John Blair
Fred Blassie
Peter Blitzer
Jim Bloom
Jack Bode
Lucas Bonnier
Gordon & Barbara Bowen
Camilla Bozzoli
Jessica Brackman
Rebecca Brackman
Mike Braden
Dan Brekke
John Brockman
Russell Brown
Neil Burgess
Patty Burness
David & Iris Burnett
Eric Burns
Stanley & Sara Burns
Brenda Buxton
Herb Caen

Woody Camp
Bill Campbell
Joseph & Janeal Cannon
Cornell Capa
Michael Castleman
Philip Castro
Frank Catchpool, M.D.
Anthony Catsimatides
Ray Cave
Mike & Gina Cerre
Howard & Jeanette Chapnick
Felicia Clark
Mike Clary
CMP Project Gulliver
Jennifer Coley
Jenny Collins
Michael Patrick Collins
David Cohen
Rob Cook
Gene Corr
Stephanie Cunningham
Ernest Cowan
Scott R. Crapo
Wendy Dale
Maura Carey Damacion
Elaine Davenport
Sashka T. Dawg
Arthur Deikman
Lou DeMatteis
Ray & Barbara DeMoulin
Robert DeVecchi
Sandro Diani
Jodi Ditto
Dana & Chris Doggett
Sheila Donnelly
David Doubilet
La famille Doutreloux
Arnold & Elaine Drapkin
Peter Drekmeier
Terri Driscoll
John Durniak
Paul Eddy
Owen & Regine Edwards
Maureen Mahon Egen
Steven Egri
Sandra Eisert
Rosemarie Ellis
Gloria Emerson
Erin Ennis
Jeannette Etheridge
Steve Ettlinger
Bill Evans
Michael Evans
Alan & Barbara Feldman
Douglas Ferguson, Esq.
George Fisher
Keith Foxe
Eleanor Naythons Freedman
David Friend
Jennifer & Mike Fuller
Josh Fuller
Selena Fuller
Ken Fund
Eduardo Fuss
John & Lynn Gage
Jamie Gangell
Rebecca Gardner
John Gianninni
Wendy Gimbel
Micke & Mary Glauser
Kate Godfrey
Mark Godfrey
Mary Margaret Goggin

Diego & Suzie Goldberg
Claire & Ray Golden
Kathy Golden
Christine Gomez
Arty & Flo Grace
Jennifer Grace
Bill Gray
Mellissa Gray
Howard Green
Bob & Kathy Gregory
Judy Griesedieck
Mary Ellen Guroy, M.D.
John & Connie Gustafson family
Carl Gustin
Don & Kristin Guy
Dana & Anna Halls
Mary Stewart Hammond
Nelson Hancock
Gary & Ann Hare
John Harkin
Acey Harper
April Star Harper
John & Karen Hendren
Matt Herron
Marty Hesterly
Harriet Heyman
Ken Heymann
Maria Hjelm
Sam Hoffman
Inger Hogstrom
Bob Holmes
Amy Horton
Carla Hotvedt
Pearl & Arnold Jacobs
Carey Johnson
Bill & Sara Joy
Devyani Kamdar
Brian Kapanoske
Ed Kashi
Jack & Honey Keating
Suzanne Keating
Tom Keller
Paul Kelly
Nick Kelsh
Tom Kennedy
David & Rebecca Kennerly
John Kifner
Doug & Francoise Kirkland
Laurence J. Kirshbaum
Kelly Kobza
Roberto Koch
Tim Koogle
Michael Kramer
J.P. & Eliane Laffont
Rupda & Vishuas Lambley
Jim Larson
Kristha Le
Jain Lemos
Michael Leonard
Carla Levdar
Larry Levitsky
John Loengard
Bill Longley
Robert Loomis
Arsenio Lopez
Richard LoPinto
Barbara Loren
Steven & Kalleen Lund
Peter Macchia
Bob & Bernadette Mack
Noam Maitless
Joan & Mike Marchitto
Nina Marinkovich

John & Leslie Markoff
David Markus
Gloria Marquez
Richard & Freda Masur
Matt Mauch
Stephanie Maze
Milton McCullough
Nion McEvoy
Anne McGrath
Richard McHenry
Liz Perle McKenna
Linda McNeil
Kevin McVey
Susan Meiselas
Charlotte "Arky" Meisner
Dorothy Mendolson
Stan Menscher
Doug & Tereza Menuez
Don Mereen
Keith & Lori Metzger
Don Meyers
Peter Miller
Phillip Moffitt
Mike Moritz
Garner Moss
Robin & Boots Moyer
Karen Mullarkey
Greg Munson
Pedro Meyer
Benjamin Naythons
Mattie Naythons
Susan Walker Naythons
William Naythons
Nanscy Neiman
Lynne Noone
Rod & Sheila Nordland
Yogi O'Kelly
Dan O'Shea
Bernard & Kate Ohanian
Daniel Okrent
Bruce & Christine Olsen
Elaine Olsen
Dean Ornish, M.D.
Mike Pagano
Gabe Perle
Brent Peterson
Kerri Pickett
Dick Pignataro
Carol Pisarczyk
Catherine Pledge
Robert Pledge
Eric Pollack
Andrew Popper
Robert Rabkin, M.D.
Sylvie Rebot
Barry Reder
Chris Reed
Stacy Reverby
Amy Rhodes
Patti Richards
Jim Richardson
Barbara Ries
Ty Roberts
Scott Rodgers
Blake & Nancy Roney
Gerald Rosenberg
John & Lynn Rosenberg
Lionel Rosenblatt
Roger Rosenblatt
Michael & Carol Rosenfeld
Trey Roski
Kitty Ross
Joe Rossi
Roy Rowan
Galen & Barbara Rowell
Michel Rudman
Barbara Runde
Kathy Ryan

Jean & the kids Saba
Paul Saffo
Cyril de Saint Hilaire
Sebastiao & Lelia Salgado
Curt Sanborn
Ellen Sanok
Laura & Roy Sardina
William Sarnoff
Joel Sartore
Kathy Saypol
Kurt Schaeffer
Aaron Schindler
Deborah Schneider
Jeff Schultz
Val Schuszer
Marion Schut-Koelemij
Thomas & Vicki Scott
William Scoville
Robert & Patti Seidman
Ruth Shapiro
Carol & Michael Sheggeby
Rosalie Sheggeby
Ron Shelton
Stephanie Sherman
Lisa Shultz
Susan Siegel
Goksün Sipahioglu
Leif & Ann Skoogfors
Angela Smith
Jeff Smith
Rod Smith
Marvin Smolan
James Spottiswoode
Roger Spottiswoode
Phyllis Springer
Dieter Steiner
George Steinmetz
Michele Stephenson
Jim Stockton
Duane Stone
Larry Stone
Summer
Mary Swanson
Homer Sykes
Arthur & Kathryn Taylor
Rebecca Taylor
Marilyn & Warren Thomas
Judith Thurman
Karen Tumulty
Della Van Hyst
Carole Vandermeyde
Kitty Veevers
Louise Velasquez
Jacque & Larry Vidal
Paul Viemester
Markku Vuorela
Jill Waldman
James Walker
Tom Walker
Walter Walker
Steve Walsh
Kate Warne
Alan Waxman
Lili Weigert
Suzanne Welch
Bill White
Diane Wildman
Preston & Dotty Williams
Alice Willson
Miriam Winocour
Katherine Withers
Sandra Wong
Edith Woodling
Kristen Wurz
Tom Young
Ed Zepernick
Patrick Zerbib

THIS BOOK WAS TYPESET IN MINION ROMAN
ON MACINTOSH COMPUTERS.
FILM PROCESSING BY COLORITE, NEW YORK.
COLOR PRINTS BY FAULKNER COLOR LABS,
SAN FRANCISCO.

Mattie Eleanor Naythons, age six months, sits for
her first Christmas portrait.
Photograph: Susan Walker Naythons